IT'S MY PARTY

A CELEBRATION OF THE ART OF EVENT DESIGN

JOE MINEO

WITH WRITING BY GARY BITNER

PREFACE

I always knew I was different. I recognized that something set me apart but I didn't always know how to articulate that the difference was creativity. I knew that I saw things differently than others around me. While there were times when that awareness made me feel detached from the world, for the majority of my 52 years, the way my mind works has given me a sense of security, confidence and happiness. Inspiration, and recognizing it, has formed and shaped my career. It's what keeps me going, personally and professionally. I pursue inspiration constantly and creatively; it keeps me on a high. The most exciting thing about inspiration is in knowing that at any moment, the smallest spark of it could turn into a magical event or an elaborate celebration.

I am also a very ambitious person. I like to achieve and I like to win. Often I jump in headfirst in pursuing a new idea or venture. Most people would say that may not be the smartest way to approach a new situation, but for me it has always worked. Making bold choices isn't something that I analyze or even think about, it is just who I am. I listen to my heart guided by the voice inside of me and I jump.

This mindset could not be more apparent than when I was 23 years old and decided to open my own floral shop with little to no experience and no business background. With a dear friend and business partner by my side, I took a leap and created Something New Floral and Events. We were a traditional local florist, but we set ourselves apart by creating out-of-the-ordinary designs. Contemporary floral design was up and coming in the '80s and we were the first shop in our area to showcase high style design, bringing clients arrangements they had never seen before.

Thirty years ago event design was not a profession. We were simply flower shops that decorated parties. A floral arrangement that was lifted off the table with a lucite rod to create height, with an assortment of votive candles placed around it, was very chic in those days. Don't get me wrong, the early beginnings hold a special place in my heart, but boy, how things have changed.

Today, I am happy, along with so many of my industry peers, to say that we were part of creating the new title of Event Professional. This was something that we cultivated and nurtured, turning a job into a career that so many are now proud to claim as their chosen profession.

As an event designer, I feel so lucky to be a part of the most important moments of people's lives. It is such an honor to have clients look back at their celebrations or important milestones and remember myself, my team, and our brand, now known as Joe Mineo Creative, associated with those special memories.

Event design is similar to interior design in that we are creating a customized environment for each client. Living in a space that has been designed for you is something that you grow into, you live with it and it becomes a part of you. As an event designer, my job is to create a space that reflects the style and personality that each client wants to represent for their particular occasion. Whether it be colorful, festive and lighthearted, or mysterious, romantic, and sexy, my job, with the help of my fantastic team, is to bring the client's vision to life. The difference is that in an event, we only have a few fleeting moments to make our impression with an environment that is inviting, evocative and memorable.

Theater has always been a big part of my life and my heart has always been drawn to the stage. Many people ask me why I am not an actor these days. While I can't even imagine at this point in my busy career, working the crazy hours that I do, what it would be like to be cast in a show and then have to attend nightly rehearsals and memorize lines, theater is still a huge part of who I am. Every event that I create is theater. I treat each party like a production and elements of theater are obvious throughout every time line. Each production includes direction and acting, scripts and cues, an eager audience, and hopefully good reviews. The pre-show is like the cocktail hour, when guests arrive and mingle with the anticipation of what is to come. The opening of the curtain is our grand entrance into the party space. Intermission is after dinner, when guests get time to interact with each other. Act two is a dance number, when people let loose and dessert is displayed. The "11 O'clock Number" is the big show stopping song and it reminds me of the event's late night snack, an unexpected surprise that always puts a smile on the faces in the audience. The final curtain is exactly that: time to recap what an amazing night it has been and take a bow.

In the following pages, my team and I hope you will recognize the creativity, inspiration, ambition and theater that are part of every event we create. I hope the book inspires you no matter who you are or what you do. I hope you see the joy we put into every event, the blood, sweat, and tears it takes to produce each one, and an appreciation that we are blessed to say, we love what we do.

It's My Party!

Published by Next Century Publishing
Las Vegas, Nevada
www.NextCenturyPublishing.com

ISBN: 978-1-68102-132-4

Printed in the United States of America

I dedicate this book to my Aunt Sarah Calderone,

who saw something in me that I didn't see in myself.

Who called me special, when I felt ordinary, and who believed

in me with her whole heart. I miss you every day.

CONTENTS

INTRODUCTION

Chances are that you picked up this book because you identified with the word "party." Perhaps you're in the midst of party planning and need a little help taking your event to the next level. Maybe you're just thinking about throwing a casual or formal get together and you need to know where to start. Or potentially, you are an event professional looking to up your game.

Event design and party planning are part science and part art. This book is not about the science part. It's not about calculating how much champagne you need for a 150-person wedding reception. It's not about identifying the timeframe for correctly mailing your party invitations. And it's not about figuring out a foolproof plan for guest parking. These are all important party planning topics, but they're not covered here.

Instead, this book is about the art of creating amazing events, and more specifically, about the importance of inspiration to the process of event design and creative party planning. In and of themselves, the event photographs and stories contained herein may provide meaningful inspiration for your future events. But that's not all. In addition, each chapter traces an inspiration path through the final production of a corresponding event. The chapters will help you understand how elaborate affairs start with simple ideas or visions, as well as the genesis for those visions. Ideally, this book will help you be more open to inspiration, which can assist you not only in party planning, but also in many creative aspects of life.

People talk about "cultivating" inspiration, as if it's something that can be nurtured from within. In reality, it is the ability to direct one's consciousness that allows us the ability to gather and use inspirations. It's more about spotting an inspiring idea and knowing how to make it work for you. Think of it as an increase in awareness of your response to your surroundings, particularly when they are new and different. Recognize the potential in appreciating your immediate environment. It's trite, but it's also true: open your eyes to the world around you.

You don't need to travel to some far off land to find inspiration for event design. Store windows at the mall can be treasure troves of visual inspiration. Inside the stores, interesting fashion or furniture design can provide cues for creativity. To keep track, use your smart phone to capture interesting visual images, then review them later. Be sure to analyze why you like something, especially noting design elements like color, pattern, texture, and scale. Apply what it was that appealed to you to your event designs.

To be inspired is a state of mind. It is an active pursuit. To begin, invest some time in studying the visual arts. Consider joining a creative class. Go to places where people are doing creative things. Check out new exhibits in the nearest art gallery. Take in a few of the latest movies, especially those with unique themes, costumes and set designs. If you watch television, pick out the shows with strong visual appeal. Be aware of cultural movements. Probably the greatest opportunity for finding inspirational content is following social media outlets that focus on style and design. Tumblr, Houzz, Pinterest, PartySlate, Colossal, and Creative Boom are a few examples of online resources that showcase a wealth of creative concepts.

Of course, some people may be more sensitive to inspiration, but there are ways to maximize your inspiration sensitivity quotient. Reduce mental clutter and increase your focus to create a pathway for wider awareness of inspirational ideas. Start by saying, "I'm going to pay attention to what attracts me." Make it a mantra and repeat it whenever you're in a place with interesting visual cues.

Be direct in identifying your goals for inspiration. Immerse yourself in evocative environments. Keep in mind that sensory perception comes via sight, sound, smell, taste and touch, and event inspiration isn't necessarily limited to what you can see. Enjoy your quest to be inspired and above all, have fun. That's what parties are all about!

IN PARTY FASHION

It is sometimes apparent, early in the event planning process, that the unique talent and personal ambitions of a client can provide the essence of a sensational special event. Focusing on that talent and ambition pays a double dividend; not only does the event come together with more meaningful, personalized content, but the client becomes emotionally invested in the event and takes an active role in its ultimate success. This dynamic is amplified if the client or special event celebrant is a young person, and therefore able to make the development of the event a learning opportunity. By welcoming his or her participation, we are able to create not only a one of a kind experience, but also to provide an avenue for the honoree to progress in his or her personal journey.

Imagine a Bat Mitzvah designed around a 13-year-old fashion prodigy with the yearning and talent to create a full production runway show of her own unique clothing designs. This transformational event quickly became a case study for client participation, as well as style setting. The runway show was the centerpiece of the party entertainment and it provided the theme that the entire event was built around.

Early in the event design process, we traveled to Manhattan, into the heart of the fashion industry, with the client, the event photographer and a professional seamster. We visited Mood fabrics, the New York fabric house made famous by the fashion design reality program "Project Runway." In addition to identifying fabrics for her designs, the client selected every button, zipper and trim piece seen in the show. The photographer captured all the pre-show activity of sketching, shopping, and sewing. The resulting photos beautifully depicted the creation of the line which would debut on the catwalk the night of the event. The editorial style images were used in a custom-designed, full-color glossy "fashion magazine," which served as the party invitation. The magazine featured the young designer at work and a behind the scenes article announcing her first runway show.

The guest of honor chooses the trim for her garment designs during a trip to Mood in NYC. This image made a perfect first impression as guests approached the place card table to receive their "VIP Fashion Show pass."

A 20-foot bar in the cocktail space represents the "dream closet" and displays some of the client's own couture pieces. The bar top is made of clear acrylic so that fashionable jewerly and accessories can be seen inside.

The cocktail hour features oversized installations that display
the tools used in garment construction. Large foam sculptures of thimbles,
pin cushions, pins, needles, buttons and scissors create focal points
among the food displays.

A dramatic installation was featured in the ballroom of this event. Our team installed an array of layered trussing units followed by several sets of staircases and walkway ramps, which connected all of the units to create a structure behind the draping on the ballroom walls. Next, five 25-foot giant white decorative frames were constructed and then hung amid the drape. Video screens were installed as the backdrop inside the frames and set to transition throughout the event. As guests entered the ballroom, the designer's logo was visible inside the frames. Guests assumed this was a printed logo until suddenly a video began to play clips of the designer sketching, selecting fabrics, and sewing in her studio. At the close of the video, the screens slowly raised within the frame to reveal living models inside them. The models were glamourous in their poses while they displayed the one-of-a-kind couture clothing creations of the guest of honor.

Lucite trays placed on clothes hangers that hung from garment racks made for a fitting sushi display.

Anticipation for the fashion show energized the ballroom entrance with taking their seats on either side of the runway. The environment is charged with a vibe that feels very much like a New York Fashion Week experience.

Professional runway models walk the catwalk. The individual outfits are created from the guest of honor's designs. The clothes were all carefully made to the exact specifications and with direction from the young designer.

Dressmaker mannequins serve as centerpieces in the ballroom. Each tabletop design was an original one of a kind creation sewn by the seamster who was hired to make the various articles of clothing used in the event. Table centerpieces in the ballroom were unique and linens were selected to coordinate with each look. The mannequins were topped off with a ribbon that was printed with the young designer's signature logo.

Custom dance floor
designed by the client herself.

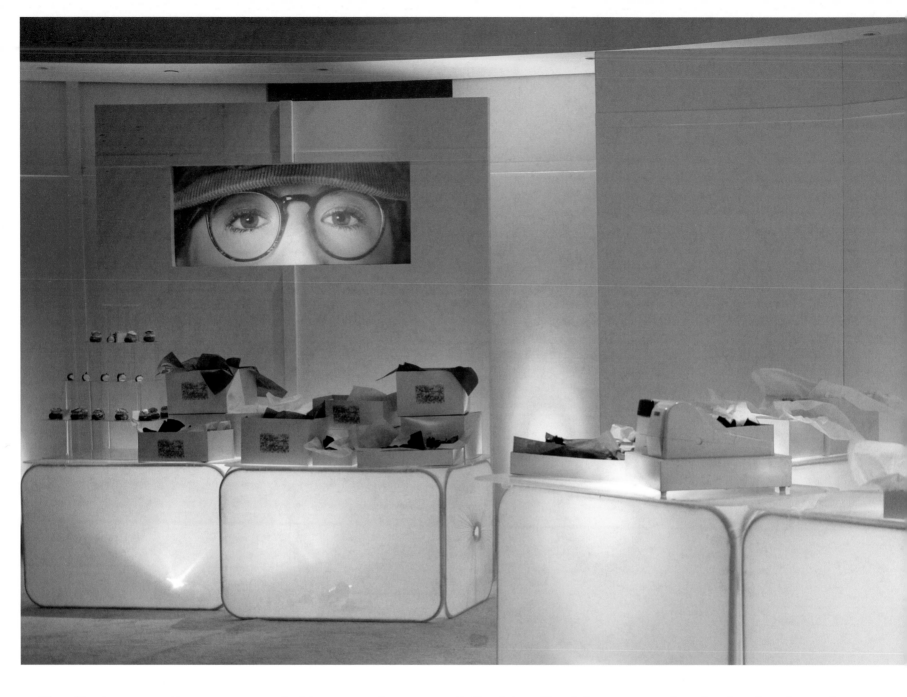

The client, as a creative person, needed to express her own artistic vision. Our job was to get into her head and turn her vision into a cohesive event theme. We needed to listen. More than listen, we needed to observe every detail of this client's personality and creative process. During the planning meetings, careful attention was paid to the personality and style of this interesting young person. In addition to absorbing what she verbally shared, we wanted to know what did she surround herself with every day, what did she read, what did she eat, and what did she watch on TV? All of these details were used to create the details of her personal milestone event. A stand out feature of the client's style - incredible eyeglasses. Every day our fashionista wore a different pair. From funky to classic, she had them all! Glasses were a personal expression of style and her way to show that she was not intimidated by design.

Eyeglasses became the inspiration for the designer's new "boutique" which was actually the display area where desserts were served. Prior to the event, a photo shoot was staged to capture images of the client modeling various pairs of her favorite signature eyeglasses. In the dessert area design, the printed photos were displayed as though they were an advertising campaign for the "boutique" and were largely featured throughout the dessert space. The food, which was presented as merchandise, was served in various shopping boxes and bags. The result was a display that was both personal and totally unique to the client. Understanding, listening, and observing creative clients leads to the greatest success in developing an event that truly represents a unique personality.

Later in the evening, guests are invited to attend the opening of the "new boutique." Costumed models act as the boutique sales associates. They present themselves as a customer service staff in a high end salon.

Desserts are displayed as merchandise in a luxury retail store. When guests make selections, their items are placed into branded shopping bags which they take back to their table and unwrap.

IN THE DRAWING ROOM

A twist on the term "drawing room" provided the inspiration for a 9-year-old's birthday party in a hand-drawn party setting. Traditional, historic references to "drawing rooms" note their initial designation as "withdrawing rooms," where guests at a private home might have been invited to "withdraw" after a formal dinner. The withdrawing room or drawing room might have then been the scene of more relaxed conversation and entertainment. Fast forward to the 21st Century and our desire to create a most unique venue to celebrate the birthday of one very special girl.

We brought the "drawing room" designation to life with actual hand-drawn design elements created and displayed throughout the party presentation. The birthday girl loved a popular children's series about a sassy little lady living in the Plaza Hotel in New York City. Celebrating amid illustrations similar to those seen in the fanciful storybook became the inspiration for this party.

We started by hiring an artist to draw original sketches from our direction. We wanted to make our own story about what this girl's life would be like if she walked into the storybook. We took the resulting drawings and blew them up to larger than life size. These were used to create faux walls, doors, curtains, and chandeliers. Literally, we were drawing the room.

The black and white of the drawing motif made a perfect backdrop for the bold stripe in the linens and chair backs. Fresh flowers extended the length of the table as speciality pastries accented each personal place setting. Delectable sweets were displayed on a three dimensional bed and drawers that jutted out from the drawings. Fresh floral floated above the table and appeared to flow out of the adorable hand drawn teapots. Books with clever titles were placed among the displays to emphasize the storybook theme. The client was just delighted with her fanciful birthday in the drawing room.

LIVING ON THE TOP FLOOR

HOW TO: HAVE A DAY that is RAWTHER FULL

SKIBBLE, SCURRY, Hop Hop Hop!

"CHARGE IT please" and "Thank you Very Much!"

Ava

Stella

Attention to detail is what makes the whimsical seem real. Personalized party hats are both decor elements but also party favors for each guest to keep. Lucite containers held the treats for the party and allowed the drawings to be the focal point.

Featuring the birthday girl's written name in the design made our little client squeal with delight. Some of the items in the drawings were representations of beloved posessions seen in photos of the guest of honor's bedroom.

GIVE THEM CHILLS

A visual spectacle of winter beauty offers visions of pure white freshly-fallen snow, clear icicles dripping in the sun and glistening ice crystals dotting bare tree branches. Together, they provide inspiration for a visually-stunning event, especially when it's a wedding in January.

The lesson here for the event designer: embrace cold weather, don't fight it. Your guests will love the sophisticated look you create with silver and white design elements; they will appreciate turning a weather worry into a visually-inspired part of their wedding celebration. Such was the case at a wedding setting we playfully labeled, "Baby, It's Cold Outside." Given the mid-winter date and the Midwest location, the theme was all too true. And yet, wedding guests loved the winter elegance created throughout the ceremony and reception spaces. This did not mean hanging plastic snowflakes from the ceiling. Cliché displays are the quickest way to turn off your sophisticated guests. Subtle hints of design always trump collections of clichés.

The wedding ceremony was treated with a little more warmth. Rather than focus on the winter theme we went the opposite direction and created an organic gazebo of twisted vines and blooming branches. An assortment of pillar candles added an element of romance while giant "snowballs" of white roses hinted at what was to come.

The reception room of silvery décor against stark black and white continued the elegant winter weather design. At the center of the ballroom was a raised platform under a tier of flowers, including white orchids, white roses and white hydrangea. Garlands of beaded crystals cascaded from the top-level of flowers. The beads helped to establish a special space for the bride and groom to enjoy the reception. Two elegant silver and white chairs featured silver wrought-iron backs that reached up and over the newly-married couple. Their centerpiece continued the white floral presentation.

Reception guests dined at tables with a combination of black and white cloth linens. Acrylic Napolean chairs featured white cushions, while tabletop displays included large beaded crystal candleholders and ornate crystal stemware. Elaborate silver chargers were graced with calligraphy place cards and menus in black and white. Low profile display boxes of cut glass held more white roses and hydrangea.Throughout the room, towering crystal centerpieces of high-profile white roses encircled by strands of beaded glass sat upon tall white tree branches. Walls were adorned with white sheer drapery, that when uplit, gave the room an ethereal glow. The shimmering crystal bar was enhanced by elaborate silver framed mirrors. Rows of beads hung to the floor from beneath the white bar countertop. One side of a 6-tiered white and black wedding cake also featured a flow of white orchids and roses from top to bottom.

It may have been cold outside, but the natural beauty of this winter wedding was sure to warm the heart of every guest.

Tables
1 - 14
←

Tables
15 - 32
→

A simple yet very tall cake with the drama of a floral garland cascading down the side of the tower sat atop a glass pedestal floating above a bed of white roses, hydrangeas and orchids.

We used two different centerpiece designs to create contrast in the decor. Mixing the two foundations, one featuring crystal orbs and the other white twig trees, made the view across the ballroom interesting.

SILVER SCREEN SOIRÉE

We always watch for clients' special interests or hobbies that intersect with visually creative worlds like art, theater, fashion, and of course, cinema. Slam dunks for inspiration and event design, these visual concepts are a hit with party guests and obviously resonate with the clients who inspire them. In this case, it's a birthday party for the guest of honor, who is a movie buff with a preference for the films from the Golden Age of Hollywood. Hence the Hollywood glam theme as part of an event we called "Legends of the Silver Screen," featuring femme fatales of the early days of cinema prominently showcased on the walls around a room designed to excite the close friends, work partners and family members of the guest of honor. Among the actress legends showcased at the event were Bette Davis, Katherine Hepburn and Marilyn Monroe, all glamorous early talents with audience appeal that crosses over multiple generations. Large black and white head shot photographs of these actresses from the Golden Age of film were framed with thousands of pieces of metallic paper, in an effect that makes the metallic paper look like thousands of miniature mirrors. Pink lighting illuminated the photographs and paper frames, adding an air of colorful sophistication and reinforcing the glamorous theme.

The party scene was all about glitter, glitz and the generous use of reflective materials. Sections of polished chrome chain hung at varying lengths from overhead chandeliers. Tall centerpieces of aluminum balls interspersed on aluminum rods also included orchid blossoms rising from arrangements of white rosebuds and green orchids. A custom bar was built to compliment the centerpiece. Glass ornaments and aluminum rods decorated the front of the bar, with glass champagne glasses lining the top of the bar and reflecting the pink light from overhead.

Acrylic tables draped with sheer linens were lit from underneath and combined with larger table rounds draped with shimmering silver and pewter striped table cloths. Acrylic floating ponds included aluminum balls and cymbidium orchids, along with white rosebuds, and were used alternately as table centerpieces. The tables were completed with white china in a silver dot pattern emanating from the center of each plate, with silver napkins folded in a round presentation and highlighted by more silver balls. Round glassware complemented the aluminum orbs suspended on the centerpiece aluminum rods. Plexiglas chairs with rounded chair backs were offset with the clean lines of simple, square back party chairs.

The scene was an ideal presentation for the Guest of Honor, who was not only a movie buff, but a "Grand Dame" and a legend in her industry. This "Legends of the Silver Screen" birthday party was one that she and her guests will long remember.

Plastic chain link was used to make the chandeliers. The high shine metallic finish read like metal but the plastic links were hollow. The finished piece was lightweight and easy to transport and hang.

INSPIRED FÊTE

Design inspiration is all around us, it's true, but it also lives within us, in terms of events and places we've previously experienced, and the memories we've captured along the way. History is also an abundant resource for design inspiration. For parties of today, sometimes the best design inspiration can come from parties of yesteryear.

Fortunately, photography was just coming into its own when elaborate gilded age social affairs were all the rage in New York, London, Paris and other turn-of-the-century metropoli. We have many detailed photographs of prominent partygoers surrounded by their gilded age accoutrements; art galleries sometimes mount shows of such stuff. These Art Nouveau-era photos point us to potential design elements for today's sophisticated event plans. Consider the classic textile pattern, known as Chinoiserie as part of an event design motif. We gained inspiration from the fanciful imagery found in the many versions of this print which came to be as the imitation or evocation of Chinese motifs and technique applied to western design. Chinoiserie was all the rage of the decorative arts world in the 18th century.

To bring Chinoiserie to life, wrought iron birdcages with live cockatiels, doves and parakeets were suspended in air around a private 20-foot by 20-foot room. Mini-versions of the birdcages decorated the guests' table, all part of a design salute to the motif. Glassware selections included cut crystal glasses passed down through the bride's family from her grandmother, as well as amber-cast wineglasses and eclectic water glasses with ridges. A combination of ornate china patterns further accented the historical party theme. Custom menus and ivory satin napkins graced the charger plates. The entire design was built upon huge wood sections of a disassembled turn-of-the-century gazebo. Two pieces were used to anchor massive floral sprays on two walls of the event space. Another was used to create the table edge; crystal teardrops hung delicately from it. The seating beneath was very eclectic, with vintage stools, benches and chairs to modernize the gilded age theme.

Floral elements included an elaborate combination of gardenias, reinculea, roses, peonies, freesia, cherry blossoms and forsythia. Multiple shades of yellow, the favorite color of the bride, were used throughout the party design. Flowers were further accented with pheasant feathers and a collage of mercury glass mixed with small stained wooden boxes, painted silver as if they were coated with mercury. To camouflage an unsightly doorway, a faux wallpaper was designed and printed to look like shelves arranged with various accoutrement; photographs, small vases, candlesticks, books, and other intricate decorative items fooled the eye. There was no limit to the interesting visual details that imprinted to memory this one-of-a-kind bridal luncheon experience.

Creative graphic design can elevate any event concept. It can also be your best friend when you need to hide an existing sign, structure or artwork in your venue. Here we used a clever "trick of the eye" technique to disguise an unsightly doorway. The printed piece does not overpower the design but adds depth to the scene while hiding an existing eyesore very effectively.

ONCE IN A LIFETIME

Most of the events showcased in this book involve spectacular parties for hundreds of guests, and, in fact, the majority of the events produced by Joe Mineo Creative have guest lists in the hundreds or thousands. While every event is unique and designed to adapt to special circumstances, we usually think in terms of quality and quantity. Not so with one special wedding.

In this case, our charge was to create a most elaborate wedding and reception for 21 guests, all extremely close friends and family members of a couple who desired to host a most extraordinary experience for a very select few. Instead of quantity, this couple wanted quality. They consciously focused on creating a magnificent experience for the people they held closest to them. The venue was the happy couple's grand home, already an elaborate venue with detailed woodwork, heirloom antiques, one-of-a-kind lighting and marble and wood flooring. Arriving guests were personally welcomed by the bride and groom in the foyer.

The ceremony took place on the landing of the grand staircase, abundantly decorated with sprays of 3,000 dendrobium orchids and 4,000 white and blush roses. The goal was to enhance the natural beauty of the wood staircase without camouflaging it. Guests were seated at the base of the lavish staircase. Behind them, the fireplace and mantle of the ballroom were adorned with massive arrangements of orchids and roses. Following the wedding ceremony, the newly-married couple welcomed their guests to a formal dinner experience at one long table. Four sterling silver heirloom candelabras were topped with huge arrangements of hundreds of white, pink, lavender and blush roses, and white dendrobium orchids all accented with ostrich feathers. The table was adorned with glass and gold-gilded china, as well as sterling silver utensils and accent pieces, including sterling silver bird sculptures anchoring lace napkins on top of charger plates. A combined menu and place card was individually inscribed with calligraphy and displayed on an easel at each place setting. One long floral arrangement stretched from end to end along the center of the formal banquet table.

Tuxedo-clad waiters in tails were assigned one to each guest. The presentation of each course was choreographed to music, all rehearsed by the waiters and kitchen team in advance of the event. Guests were entertained during the meal by a pianist on grand piano and accompanied by a bass guitarist. The formal nine course meal began with a first course choice of cream of asparagus soup with crème fraiche or parmesan tuile wafer and chives. Course two included coquille St. Jacques with diver scallops, mushrooms, white wine, cream and gruyere in shell with rock salt. The salad course featured mixed greens with red and yellow watermelon and fried goat and gourgeres cheese. Each course was presented on unique china. The main course included a trio plate of beef wellington with port wine sauce, parmesan crusted veal tenderloin medallion with sautéed spinach and a pistachio-crusted double-bone lamb chop with sweet pea and mint risotto. The meal ended with the cutting of the tufted fondant wedding cake set into a sterling silver cake pedestal accented with florals and topped with a sculpture of small birds, all surrounded by votive candles and floral sprays.

After an intimate and moving ceremony and a delectable meal, departing guests each received an individually-selected and unique gift that was personally presented by the newly-married couple. The gifts will always be a reminder of a most unforgettable wedding – truly a once-in-a-lifetime experience.

The couple wanted to incorporate their pet cat into their ceremony. We tied the wedding rings to the cat's collar with satin ribbon, but not too tight so that the groom could retrieve them easily. Unfortunately, the cat did not want to go down the stairs on cue; when we got him to go down, the ribbon came loose and the rings went rolling down the staircase. It was W.C. Feilds who said, "Never work with children or animals."

Garlands of greenery hung on the staircase as a foundation for the fresh flowers, tucked in using a very light hand.
The completed garlands had a delicate cascading effect. We wanted to accent, not overpower, the beauty of this spectacular staircase.

Beautiful brides with exquisite taste are a dream come true for any event designer. While this bride was involved in the creative process, she trusted us fully to bring her vision to life. It was truly a pleasure to design this special day for her and her new husband.

A vintage style sheer silk fabric bejeweled with aurora borialis crystals and finished with the application of individually placed satin rosettes gave the custom-made linen and chair covers an heirloom quality.

Trusted partners are invaluable for flawless execution of an event. For this wedding, we worked with a favorite chef to create a delicious and beautifully presented menu.

The cake exemplifies our theme with lush florals made of sugarpaste and a Lladro sculpture topper.

IT'S ABOUT TIME

Subcultures can provide creative inspiration and huge visual impact. Grunge. Goth. Zombie. Punk. Fringe subcultures are treasure troves of inspiration because of their unique combinations of visual and design elements often communicated through fashion and music. They are frequently the springboard for emerging artists, whose new works reinforce and grow the impact of the subcultural movements from which they were inspired. An outstanding example of capturing such subculture trends is Madonna. From her 1990 "Justify My Love" track, with its connection to a sadomasochism subculture, to the huge dance hit "Vogue," inspired by the Harlem Vogue scene in the late 1980s, and many more songs and shows both before and since, Madonna has built an entertainment empire based on the creative impetus captured from the careful study of cultural movements. She reinterpreted many of them into mainstream hits and has delivered waves of new enthusiasts to every subculture she has touched.

For event designers, the trick is to identify such subcultures and exploit them. It was the steam punk subculture that gave rise to one of the most unique events in the history of Joe Mineo Creative, when we fashioned an "It's About Time" program to commemorate the 125th Anniversary of Children's Hospital of Pittsburgh of UPMC, on behalf of the client, Children's Hospital of Pittsburgh Foundation. The Foundation approached us well before the proposed anniversary program; they had not held a similar event for more than 10 years and wanted to resurrect the historied gala in a big way. As a result, the "It's About Time" inspiration took on multiple meanings; it referred to the many years that the organization served its community and also teased at the decade that the gala had been absent from the Pittsburgh social calendar. In the event itself, the title connected to both a visual interpretation of time and time pieces, and also imparted a sense of urgency to the evening's festivities, which included welcome cocktails, dinner and a program to showcase multiple successes of Children's Hospital.

Steam punk is a rich mix of Victorian-era visuals with futuristic machine elements, as well as an industrial connection that allowed us to visually acknowledge the rich manufacturing history of Greater Pittsburgh and its importance to the 125-year evolution of Children's. Think clocks, machines and metals mixed with cut crystal and lace – that's the picture. Giant timepieces and clock parts loomed large as 900 arriving guests entered the venue, with a welcoming display of huge vinyl window graphics and modern colors of white, violet and silver. Escalators added to the mechanical theme, thanks to spinning metal arrangements that alternately threw light and shadows around the corridor walls and ceiling. At check in tables, upside down tulip displays contrasted cleverly with the wide view of downtown Pittsburgh seen through huge plate glass windows.

Confronted with a suspended glass walkway of more than 100 feet between the cocktail space and grand ballroom, we opted to make the entire walkway part of the party, placing bars at either end with visual elements, food and seating within the walkway. On the floor below, scenes of performance art played out to the delight of arriving guests. These included spotlit dancers whose synchronized movements brought the "It's About Time" theme to life. Along the way, guests encountered actors in steam punk costumes and body paint of industrial designs.

First impressions are so important, and yet so brief. Often the need to transform an entrance can be overlooked in an effort to keep the decor focused on the areas where guests will spend the most time. In this case, where we were presented with many questions about the appropriateness of hosting such an important event in a convention center venue, we needed to own the space from the start. We used temporary window graphics to brand the first impression of our event in a dramatic way. The moment guests entered the huge building, they immediately began to experience "It's About Time."

GIVE KIDS A CHANCE TO BE KIDS

125 YEARS of CARING

We hire our own photographer for high profile events giving them strict instructions to capture photos of attendees or entertainers as they experience the event. The resulting images of visually interesting people interacting with the event design enhances the impression left long after the event is over.

Place cards put guests at ease. They impart a sense of security and attention to detail. When assigned their seat, guests know that they have a place to put their belongings and that they can immediately start to enjoy themselves. In events that don't use cards, it is common to see guests anxiously trying to find the best view or location in the room. Another issue that assigned seating avoids is the potential for negative interactions caused by seat saving.

In order to make a strong statement in a vast space, we turned the centerpieces upside down. Thousands of French tulips were hung from circular structures suspended over the tables.

Event actors are costumed elaborately to complement the steam punk inspired time theme. An airbrush makeup artist added industrial and mechanical elements by applying metallic body paint designs.

The actors stood out from the crowd and were helpful in moving the guests from the cocktail space into the ballroom.

The fact that our ceiling design included a broken clock face worked to our advantage. We were able to print the individual pieces affordably while still presenting the illusion of having created one enormous clock. The metallic material that was printed upon caught the light and glowed in the vast space beautifully.

The multi-story back wall of the grand ballroom featured three giant 40-foot high screens of video projection. The wallpaper pattern, which was initially static, on cue from the cellists, began to peel. A gong chimed and behind the wallpaper a giant clock face character called The Timekeeper was revealed on the center screen. This custom animation came to life and verbally welcomed arriving guests, who were already enjoying the sounds of a rock cello trio, combining Victorian-era musical instruments with music of today at the center of the ballroom dance floor.

A ceiling reveal showcased a dozen huge glowing clocks as well as parts from one massive gold metal clock that had broken apart and scattered overhead pieces as large as eight by eight feet. As mechanized music grew louder, spotlights landed on the seven performers of Cirque Mechanics, who pedaled their huge metal gantry bike over VIP guests at center tables and into position above the dance floor, where they performed a series of acrobatic feats to complement the "It's About Time" theme of the evening. Seated at their tables, guests discovered the evening's menu printed on a large clock wheel and lush floral tablescapes, with lemon leaf stands over intricate gold tablecloths, gold candleholders and candles, gold vases full of flowers and gold table settings. The elaborate set up paved the way for the evening's extraordinary program created to inspire support throughout the community. "It's About Time" was reviewed as one of the most spectacular events ever presented in Pittsburgh, and one that will always be remembered by the guests who were there to experience it.

Custom bars are a way to keep your events one of a kind. It can be expensive and time consuming to design and construct unique structures that look like permanent fixtures but it is an essential component to any high profile event.

Another aspect of a successful client experience is proper training of the service staff. A meeting is scheduled to go over a handout that includes the do's and don'ts of proper white glove service as well as possible challenges to the timeline or flow of the meal. This preparation in advance reinforces the highest quality service standards and insures that any issues that arise are handled properly.

Entertainment by Cirque Mechanics was chosen to accent our theme. We are always on the lookout for acts that can delight and surprise guests with the unexpected. Word to the wise: always customize any entertainment performance. Acts often have set routines that they use in a variety of settings. What is crucial for any event designer or producer to remember is that the timing of big moments in a routine need to be tweaked. Timing is everything and what works for an act in their own arena can be devastatingly slow or out of sync when plugged into an event timeline. Even if you have seen an act and know its quality, a good designer must always think of the entertainment and the timing of it specific to each event.

UNLIKE ANY OTHER

Weddings are so often all about tradition. From the invitations to the rehearsal and rehearsal dinner, to the ceremony and reception, many wedding components are often planned purely to fit a traditional model.

Enter a bride-to-be who wants to do things differently, and who has exquisite taste, and the outcome can be quite spectacular: a wedding that breaks the rules and yet maximizes the experience of the wedding party and their guests. It helps to know which rules to break, without diminishing the experience of family members, especially the mother of the bride, who may cling to traditional wedding plans. In this case, a wedding planner may also need to play the role of mediator, finding ways to compromise to help all parties achieve the finest possible event. There can be a tenuous balance between foregoing convention yet honoring tradition that if achieved can exceed the vision of the clients. One of our recent weddings played out with a bride-to-be who pushed the limits of tradition, yet respected her family's involvement and carefully considered their viewpoints. It began with the wedding invitation, which was written traditionally, but printed on a Plexiglas square and delivered atop a dupioni silk pillow that was fitted into a fabric covered gift box. The gift box was secured with a wide ribbon and topped with a handmade paper orchid. This atypical invitation presentation set the tone for an unconventional event.

The traditional Catholic wedding service was held in the family's church, which allowed us to transform the worship hall with specially-fabricated, 13-foot silk trees. Four of the trees were positioned on the altar and eight were interspersed among the pews to bring the outdoors in. This added a natural beauty to an already striking wedding venue. The inspiration for this came from the wedding designer for Prince William and Kate Middleton, who created a similar scene for their nuptials at Westminster Abbey. The cocktail party before the reception took place at the foot of a grand staircase decorated with hundreds of giant paper roses, ranging in diameter from 18 to 30 inches. In addition to creating an exceptional visual impact for the cocktail decor, the grand staircase of giant paper roses provided a one-of-a-kind backdrop for memorable wedding photographs. Based on the bride's wishes, the evening timeline was intentionally blurred between the cocktail party and the reception; guests were encouraged to move from one to the other as they wished.

The wedding reception was elaborate and unique. A combination of table shapes and sizes invited guests to dine wherever they preferred, with some enjoying the event at high top tables while others preferred casual seating at various combinations of sofas and loveseats. The setup encouraged relaxed informal interaction among wedding guests. A few of the furniture groupings spilled out onto the high-gloss dance floor. Table centerpiece décor was anything but casual and included a variety of Lucite candleholders and tall supports used as the bases for elaborate arrangements and sprays with pink, yellow and orange florals that draped over the sides of the centerpiece stands.

Ceilings draped with flowing fabric supported massive white chandeliers of white sheer and satin ribbons along with cascades of white phalaenopsis orchids. Bar backsplash units were decorated with large vertical mirrors interspersed with sconces of matching floral topiaries. For dessert, the wedding cake display presented another break from tradition. Multiple cakes which were the request of the bride, none of them typical wedding cakes, in many different flavors, were arranged as a beautiful alternative to the norm. These confections were accompanied by a variety of gourmet pastries arranged on the branches of dessert "trees," decorated with white hydrangeas.

Unique, different, avant-garde and event daring, this was one wedding that broke a few rules and, as a result, is completely unforgettable.

MR. AND MRS. JOSEPH KEROLA
REQUEST THE HONOUR OF YOUR PRESENCE
AT THE MARRIAGE OF THEIR DAUGHTER

Maggie Marie
TO
Brian Earl

SON OF MR. WAYNE COX AND
MR. AND MRS. WILLIAM BRUGGEMAN
SATURDAY, THE NINETEENTH OF JULY
TWO THOUSAND AND FOURTEEN
AT ONE THIRTY IN THE AFTERNOON
ST. PATRICK'S CHURCH
357 N MAIN STREET HUBBARD, OHIO
FORMAL ATTIRE

Visually impressive from beginning to end. The wedding invitation was printed on Lucite, foreshadowing the decor design.

This dramatic photo of the venue exterior was taken after our lighting designer illuminated the prestigous and historic building. It offered a wonderful last look as guests left the reception venue.

It is important to address existing objects of a venue to make the space more personal. Here, we added a thick ring of fresh hydrangea blooms to accent the fountain in the center of the cocktail area.

The bride's gorgeous bouquet was made up of Free Spirit roses, Phalaenopsis orchids, Cattleya orchids, Purple Anemone, and Green Trick dianthus.

Spectacular centerpieces towered over tables atop acrylic rods. A lush band of exotic floral comprised of mini calla lilies, Phalenopsis orchids, roses, hydrangea and weeping amaranthus divided the upper and lower sections of rods.

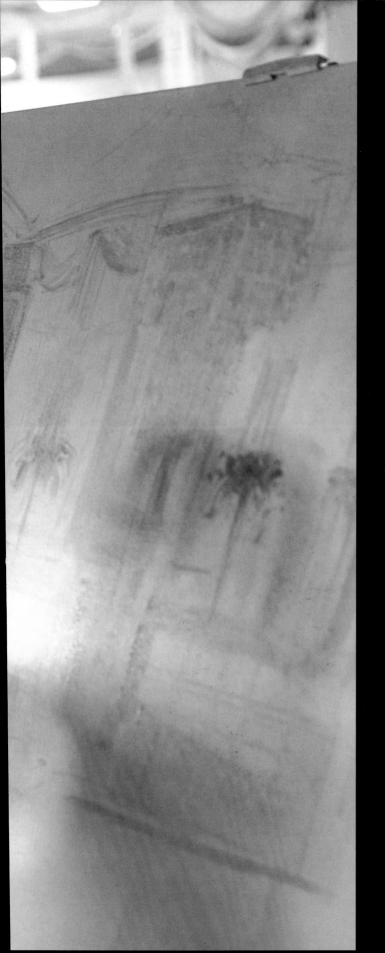

Why not have the late night snack passed by some eye candy?

A wonderful surprise to the bride and groom was the artist that painted the reception as it was happening. The finished piece was a special gift from the bride's mother and father.

We approach the design of each event thinking of what areas will become great photo oppurtunities. Not only do the clients and the professional photographer appreciate having a variety of backdrops, but now that everyone has a cell phone with a camera, guests enjoy taking selfies amid the decor.

GAME ON

Every potential theme for an event has just that: potential. No matter how common the proposed concept, the potential is always there to take an often used idea and turn it into something special. Clients with teenage boys or girls frequently suggest a birthday, mitzvah or graduation celebration based on a sports theme reflecting the honoree's athleticism and interest in all things sports. The young person's focus may be on sports participation or attendance at sporting events, or a combination of both. It's rarely appropriate for an event designer to change a client's mind, no matter how similar the proposed theme might be to a dozen other parties held the same season. Instead, we take it as a challenge to create once-in-a-lifetime experiences out of even the most popular of event themes. How, then, to reinvent the sports party into something new and different?

It starts with the event invitation arriving in a logo branded tin filled with popcorn and topped by an embroidered baseball cap complete with retail style hang tags that outlined the Mitzvah project in a "Nike Ad" inspired design. Inside the tin, the invited guests found the printed invitation ticket as well as an authentic pack of baseball cards, complete with bubble gum, that featured the action sports photos and stats of the celebrant.

The arrival experience is a critical first impression for attendees. In this case, we outfitted our valet drivers in referee uniforms and instructed them to use hand signals and whistles to communicate as guests pulled up. From there guests were ushered to an entrance display of chain link fence, turf and popping popcorn from which place cards on dowel rods and designed as game tickets could be seen. The cocktail area was busy with activity to entertain any age sports enthusiast. We brought in a bevy of video and live play games: race car simulators, free throw basketball stations, foozball, and a motor cross themed green screen photo op just to name a few. A cocktail bar for adults was adorned with hundreds of baseballs and plastic baseball bats spray-painted silver, along with vintage baseball pennants. Décor textures included scrunched up aluminum screening and even the sports-oriented chain link fence, with industrial blue lighting to enhance the décor's aluminum look.

In the ballroom, balls from every sport populated the event space, along with boogie boards and a custom dance floor designed to represent water for wakeboarding and applied as a peel and stick. Cardboard silhouettes of atheletes of basketball, baseball and soccer hung above food stations. Table rounds were capped with metallic paper, edged with the honoree's name and blinking LED lights. Spinning centerpieces, spinning in both directions, combined a variety of sports equipment with inspirational sports messages, such as, "The more you sweat in practice, the less you bleed in battle." Desserts were revealed in a locker room display filled with sports themed treats. A typical theme: maybe. A typical presentation: definitely not.

The invititation had multiple components that detailed specific event information. The branded popcorn tin arrived stuffed with popcorn and an embroidered hat, complete with retail type hang tags, which included info about the Mitzvah project. Inside was a pack of custom designed baseball cards, complete with bubble gum and featuring real sport stats about the honoree. The details of the after party were presented as a ticket to enter the sporting event. All the printed materials featured the logo of this party which was inspired by the trend of major retail chains creating their own "Athletic Departments."

The foyer design was very much on theme but was presented in a sophisticated way. A collage of the guest of honor involved in various sports made a graphically interesting wallpaper for the facade. The inexpensive balls that were strung on fishing line were amazing when lit and appeared to float in front of the reflection in the windows.

Valet drivers were outfitted as referees to give guests a first and final impression that was decidedly sport oriented.

Custom centerpieces were designed and manufactured using mostly acrylic components. Large boxes were made to sit on their point and spin. They were perfect, until we had to find turners that would spin weight up to 75 pounds. Something that seemed simple turned into a real challenge.

Foam silhouettes of the sports featured in "The Athletic Department" were cut and mounted as a wall piece that made for a dramatic focal point.

Twelve giant chandeliers hung throughout the ballroom. They were made of lightweight Papier–mâché balls. The scale of these chandeliers filled the negative space between the centerpiece and ceiling.

Custom graphics played a big part of the design of this event. From the "Austin" brand wake boards that lined the DJ facade to the water theme dance floor with his first name spelled out boldly across it, there was no doubt who we were celebrating. During the initial design meetings we asked the client's mother for photos of the young athlete involved in his many physical activities. It was the sheer number of sports Austin participated in and the tons of photos taken throughout his childhood that made us realize that the best way to celebrate this individual was to feature his abilities prominently throughout the party. Huge custom banners were designed to cover architectural details of the venue that did not complement the sports theme. The peel and stick dance floor, a reference to water sports, actually looked wet and gave guests a surreal feeling as they danced on top of water.

The client and I agreed that we wanted to avoid any formal meal presentation because we felt it was not appropriate to the theme. The challenge was that with over 500 confirmed guests, the space in the ballroom was already maxed out. Food stations would not be an option because there would be no room for them, let alone the lines of waiting guests.

Our solution was to plan a family-style meal that would be served on large platters and placed on a lazy susan in the center of each table. Guests could serve themselves very easily and with just a touch, spin to the next dish. We designed the structure and raised it about six inches to be at eye level. This allowed guests to easily reach over the glassware on the table. Guests enjoyed the unexpected serving style and we have used the structures many times since.

We created a fun and unexpected dessert reveal as a surprise element of this party. A colorful version of a locker room was built to display the many sweet treats that were offered. Cookies in the lockers and doughnuts on the benches were playfully decorated in sports themes.

ROCK THE PARTY

Members and supporters of the world's music elite gather in Cleveland, Ohio, every third year for the Induction Ceremony of the Cleveland-based Rock and Roll Hall of Fame. Imagine throwing a party that must dazzle 1,400 rock music aficionados, many of whom frequently experience elaborate concerts and events. Imagine organizing and presenting a memorable dinner in no more than 75 minutes, in order to meet a strict production schedule for an HBO taping of the Induction Ceremony. That's the challenge we have faced for Cleveland's last three such events. It's an honor to be selected for the design and execution of an event that supports the Rock and Roll Hall of Fame.

It's a thrill to help make history as performers like Ringo Starr, The "5" Royales, The Paul Butterfield Blues Band, Green Day, Joan Jett & the Blackhearts, Lou Reed, Stevie Ray Vaughan & Double Trouble, and Bill Withers are inducted into this prestigious cadre of musical legends. The venue, Cleveland's Public Auditorium, dictates much of what we do. The historic event space features a maze of inter-connecting function rooms. We planned them to work together as a series of musically-themed event spaces, pulling guests along a musical pathway that formed the backdrop for a dinner that flows from room to room. Our design motif began in the lobby of the Auditorium, with welcome kiosks featuring large photographs of previous inductees. From there, guests entered the inter-connecting function rooms.

Consider the five function rooms as a blank canvas, and it's our job to make them each special and integral to an overarching musical celebration theme. We opted for five themes: jazz/blues, punk, disco, rock 'n' roll and the fifth room to highlight the 30th Anniversary of the Inductions. Each room was branded with a giant image that was representative to the musical style of the room. The punk room included air brushed table cloths, floral centerpieces decorated with aluminum spray paint cans, and a custom bar display of 2,750 spray paint cans, as well as 900 spray paint cans suspended from the ceiling. The jazz/blues room featured a glamorous nightclub environment, with leaded and beaded glass chandeliers and room color accents of blue and teal. Highlights of the rock room were 10-foot long carved guitar centerpieces and custom chain chandeliers. The anniversary room was gilded in gold and featured three video screens showcasing video clips from previous induction ceremonies.

The stunning stage and screen production by HBO inspired the design of the guest tables.

2015
ROCK & ROLL
HALL OF FAME
INDUCTION CEREMONY

Guests made dinner choices at interactive food stations in each of the themed rooms, with transitional dinner seating for 1,400 people that included high-top tables and lounge furniture. Strict fire safety regulations at Cleveland's Public Auditorium meant that no food could be cooked on site, and no Sterno or other warming tools were allowed, which presented a unique challenge to event chefs. Their solution: to create a quality dinner menu without hot food items, but with memorable delicacies.

To control the crowd flow and ensure that each room was appropriately filled, we used models who were outfitted in glamorized black tie attire and further accessorized with a very purposeful 12-foot tall staph topped with a light. The models were placed in a configuration along the path so that their physical presence created a directional line. When the first guests arrived they were instructed to follow the line of lights which were easily spotted high above the crowd. As each room filled to the desired capacity, the models were directed to change their formation, thus directing the flow into the next desired space.

Following dinner, the models also led guests into the Music Hall at Cleveland Public Auditorium, site of the actual Induction Ceremony. Individual desserts were served to guests at Music Hall tables, which also featured displays of antipasto, caviar and nuts for guests to enjoy through the course of the five hour induction program. Table décor mirrored the stage design, where a pyramid theme reflected the architectural signature pyramid of the Rock and Roll Hall of Fame Museum. Guests of the Rock and Roll Hall of Fame Induction Ceremony raved about the décor and displays, likening the event to a concert spectacular, with an entire event venue transformed, like magic. We dazzled. We mesmerized. We created a most memorable event.

A favorite room of the guests was the Punk Rock Room. We considered graffiti representative of punk rock and used it to inspire the decorations, thus the 3,500 spray paint cans. Notice the use of a single item repeated to make a big visual impact. We used the cans as a ceiling treatment, as the facade and back of the bar, and also as centerpieces placed in groupings atop custom graffiti table linens.

Images selected to honor the various genres of rock sang the song of this design. Each room featured one strong image that represented modern music. Notice that the pattern in the microphone shown in the photo is repeated in the hanging chandeliers.

Our tribute to the Blues came in a shades of teal, purple and blue combined with a bold black and white fabric. Vintage chandeliers and crystal orbs in groupings gave the room another strong design feature.

Eight foot tall guitars were made of lightweight insulation, then painted and covered in fabric. A variety of bold patterns and textures were used to create the edgy rock 'n' roll attitude that the room needed.

The rock room took its design cue from the hair bands of the '80's. A wild mix of leopard, zebra and red leather, complete with some chain link chandeliers, made this an incredible, sexy party space.

The disco room was full of movement provided by the many disco balls spinning from the ceiling. The prominant image in the space referenced the disco dance era perfectly.

LIFE CHANGING EVENT

There is a moment in every successful career when it is time to grow. This can mean growth not only as a designer but also as a business. The urge to grow happened for me at a time when my company was flourishing. My business had earned the reputation for being the best florist and event designer in my hometown of Youngstown, Ohio. We were enjoying our position as the big fish in a small pond. It was a wonderful thing to see the results of the hard work pay off by being at the top of the market. The situation changes because ultimately, as designers, we not only look for the next big thing, but we want to become the next big thing. An opportunity to do this presented itself when a new client approached us to design and produce their dream wedding outside our local area. Presenting my work to a high profile audience in a metropolitan market was going to be a huge challenge, but it was time to grow. The expectations were high and we knew we had to deliver. Did I mention that I love a challenge?

I had to sit down and evaluate how my business needed to change for growth. I knew that as a designer, I was up to the challenge, but I also knew that the greatest obstacle was not the designing of a spectacular event, but in producing it. When approaching a growth opportunity event, the first thing to analyze is staff. Do you have the team that you need to plan and produce a "next level" event? There is nothing worse than having your big budget client feeling that their event is not getting the attention it deserves. This can easily happen if you try and conduct business as usual. We designate one team member to "hand hold" each client. This delegation allows the client a personal connection and sense that their event is always a priority.

Beyond planning and designing, having the right staff during the installation, running the event and even the tear down is not only important for ensuring a happy client, but can also make or break your relationships with peer vendors. As you move into a new territory or market, you want to make sure you have a staff that can communicate effectively and represent your company well. Future success and referrals so often depend on the relationships and rapport built between peer businesses. As I prepared to grow for this particular event, I looked to my peers for a variety of reasons. They were instrumental in giving me information about the venue and in warning me of any logistical issues that I needed to be aware of. My success in this event itself, as well as my ability to break into the new market was due in part to my peer vendors and the relationships I am so thankful to have with them.

Events that stand the test of time by surpassing current trends or common themes are the hallmarks of a successful design career. A perfect example of such an event was of one of our most stunning weddings, which was a tented, outdoor ceremony at a prominent country club, followed by an opulent ballroom reception. The bride had grown up in and around the country club where she, along with many of her friends and family members, shared wonderful memories. They were determined to celebrate this wedding at the venue that was so special to them. With the ballroom capacity maxed out by a guest list of 200, the only option for a separate ceremony space was a tent to be raised nearby.

Picking one ballroom or indoor venue over another is fairly straightforward. Selection is based on location, décor, capacity, food quality, reputation, and of course, cost. Erecting a tent, however, and pulling together every needed element to accommodate a high end event inside it is quite another thing. Tent venues can be complicated and costly. They require careful planning and coordination. The big advantage is flexibility; tents can be erected almost anywhere. There is no substitute for walking around a property as part of the tent site selection process, in order to consider all the logistical concerns like running utilities, loading concerns, obstacles, and traffic flow as well as to identify special equipment needs. Often, the decision of where to locate a tent comes down to picking the best view, or views, which should be a key focus of any site selection process.

As we toured the venue on my first visit with the client, we immediately knew where to place the ceremony tent: directly on the perfectly manicured golf course. We knew tents were not allowed but we presented our request for permission to the club management anyway; the immediate answer was a curt refusal. Ultimately, persistence paid off and after some collaboration with the tent company, a plan was devised to raise the tent floor and install fans around the floor perimeter. The fans circulated air over the grass during the four day installation and event itself. Special supports were constructed which ensured stability of the structure. This had never been done before and was a unique solution to protecting the golf course greens. Once approval to erect a tent was issued, the exact site for the wedding ceremony was determined. Perfectly positioned to maximize sight lines across multiple directions of the country club's beautiful grounds, when it later went up, the tent was more glorious than we had even imagined it could be. Set atop a slight hill, the tent looked stunning against the skyline. From inside, we noticed an unexpected benefit of the lifted floors: they made the visibility looking out even more spectacular. The sides of the tent were left open, taking advantage of both the panoramic views and the cool breezes.

After overcoming the issues of logistics, we began to get to know more about the clients and their personal style. It became very apparent that the bride and her mother both had exquisite taste. What a pleasure it was to work with them in creating a décor design that brought their combined vision to reality. Our goal was to elicit a feeling of romance in each guest. On wedding day, the awestruck reactions from attendees were proof that we had achieved it. The interior of the tent was made luxurious by hundreds of yards of gathered Dupioni silk, expertly draped to cover the interior tent ceiling and walls. Roman-inspired columns, originally suggested by the bride herself, were positioned in the four corners of the raised stage to create the base of the huppah. Thousands of roses and hydrangeas encircled the columns in a spiral effect.

Suspended votive candles lit the ceremony stage and added to the enchanting décor. With their expectations set high, guests proceeded to the country club ballroom, where a romantic glow radiated from candle light flickering above the splendid setting that had been created for the wedding reception. Custom designed double-tier chandeliers of pink roses, candles and glass accents towered above guest tables. Custom imported lace linens covered reception table tops. Beaded tulle chair covers laced up the back like ballerina slippers above tulle skirts, which gave the impression that the chairs floated. The bride and her family envisioned an elegant, enchanting, and romantic wedding decor. They hoped for a wedding fantasy come true. It was their vision and attention to the finest detail that set the tone of our collaboration in creating a classic event that stands the test of time.

Custom two-tier chandelier structures and tall candlesticks wrapped in strands of pearls were created for the tablescapes. We wanted the structures used in this wedding design to be one of a kind. It is challenging to find vessels that other designers are not using, so we created our own.

It's all in the details! The details are where you can differentiate yourself as a designer. Personal touches that make the day more special for your client are worth the extra effort and can start life long relationships. Here, you can see that we make an elegant tag for each bridesmaid bouquet. This little nicety makes a simple part of the wedding day very special and personal.

In the Beginning
A Raspberry and Walnut-stuffed Bosc Pear with
Peppercorn-crusted Goat Cheese on a bed of fresh
Micro Greens laced with Raspberry Walnut
Vinaigrette

Intermezzo
Assorted Citrus Sorbet Cones

Main Course
Roasted Pretzel-crusted Wild Salmon
and
Beef Tenderloin with a Mustard Morel Sauce
built on top of a Potato Tower finished with
Fried Spinach Greens

Sweet Endings
Wedding Cake
of Stephanie & Gregg's
Desserts

IT'S MY PARTY

The title of this book, "It's My Party," could be interpreted in several ways and they all make sense. It could be taken to mean, "It's Your Party," since many readers will be seeking ideas and inspiration for a party they may be planning. Or it could be a more broad reference to the "My" in "It's My Party," with each of the respective party hosts taking ownership of the parties which are showcased here. It could be a historical reference to the huge hit song by the late Lesley Gore, who took the tune "It's My Party" to the top of the pop music chart in 1963 and made the phrase so memorable. Or, it could mean that it's the author's party, and in the case of this chapter, that would be right.

On the next several pages, please consider yourself an invited guest to my recent birthday party, an over-the-top event which ballooned to nearly 400 guests. My personal thanks to each and every one of them for joining in the celebration. The life of an event planner is both a blessing and a curse. Our expertise and our contacts give us the tools to create extraordinary events. Of course, that means our guests also come with high expectations. And hopefully, at my birthday party, they weren't disappointed. You may not have realized it, but blue is my favorite color and there was plenty of blue. My favorite band entertained; they're an 11-piece troupe called Studio E that plays high energy tunes from multiple eras. Bottom line: when you're planning your own party, make it personal. Pull inspiration from within. It will be more fun for you and for your guests, who will feel a personal connection to you. Because this was a Joe Mineo birthday party, it of course came with a dose of drama, in the form of good friends who were also ballroom dancers, and who treated party guests to a competitive-level ballroom dance presentation. In addition, stunning female and male models wore display cases of seafood on ice hung from straps around their necks. The models strolled among party guests, who were invited to sample the seafood treats.

There were also doses of whimsy and humor, including two Joe Mineo life-size cutouts set up as photo props for party guest selfies. Décor design was both casual and elegant, offering table seating interspersed with groupings of lounge chairs. Linens included blue striped table cloths and runners with blue and white geometric patterns. Guests first enjoyed a reception area with multiple hors d'oeuvres stations that were replenished throughout the evening. This setup added more space and flow options to help cope with an overflow crowd. Centerpieces included 12-foot high artificial trees with thousands of individually-crafted leaves. Multiple glass orbs were suspended from each tree and held votive candles. Other tables featured centerpieces made of a combination of clear vertical tubes with a mix of white lilies, red roses, orchids and tulips. A wide bar setup was enhanced by backdrops that showcased combinations of decorative plates. Backlit drawings highlighted the bases of each of the bar stands, including caricatures of – you guessed it – Joe Mineo. The bottom line: a very personal party presentation that hopefully left guests feeling, "Wow, that was sooo Joe Mineo."

Again, you see that we have made my service staff prominent. Look at this welcoming committee! Because they were included as a part of this event, not just as an invisible workforce, they were invested in its success. My prep time with them is worth every second and

Even for eating, some guests prefer casual seating arrangements to a traditional table setting. We often combine both options, allowing guests to choose what they like. This makes the party feel casual and relaxed, as well as adding more visual interest to the room.

The tables were designed so that guests were seated under the canopy of a 12-foot green tree that grew out of a hole cut out of the center of the table. Glass votives were hung from the branches. The effect was lovely.

Outstanding floral arrangements were striking in vesslels that illuminated. Two narrow tables were set side by side leaving a 6-inch space between them. An acrylic pond filled with aluminum balls, glass vases and orchids was set over the space and then lit from below. The light shining up made the floating ponds glow.

Humourous book covers that referenced aging were printed for stacks of books which were placed amid the decor where guests could get a laugh out of them. Centerpieces were created using Loamy tubes. They make a unique foundation for modern floral design. Loamy tubes are lightweight, easily glued and inexpensive.

**CEDAR ROASTED HERB
CRUSTED SALMON**

GREEN BEAN, CUCUMBER & ONION SALAD
COUS COUS
CABBAGE, CUCUMBER & CARROT SLAW
AND LIME MUSTARD SAUCE

CARVED ROASTED TURKEY

CARAMELIZED BUTTERNUT
SQUASH & BRUSSELS SPROUTS
CRANBERRY ORANGE RELISH
DRIED CHERRY PEAR KETCHUP

The caterer, a dear friend and colleague,
did an incredible job of designing a menu
around all of my favorite foods.

Family and friends truly make life rich in a way money never can. I am blessed. My birthday party was designed by me but was filled (behind my back) with so many surprises and personal touches. Speeches, gags, video messages, and performances showered love upon me throughout the night. It was one of the most personal and touching events I have ever attended.

Many of my favorite event industry peers came together to make the party extra special for me. The photo op was provided by Rock the House Entertainment.

My friends from The Fred Astaire Dance Studio surprised me with a sizzling dance number that blew everyone away.

LOCAL FLAVOR

Trendy. The word implies overuse and perhaps a lack of sophistication. In design, the implication of "trendy" might be a bit negative, as if designers should know better than to jump on a current style bandwagon. When it comes to inspiration, trends can be a starting point. It's the responsibility of the event designer to analyze and understand a trend, in order to take it to a higher level and present design components that are unique, interesting and captivating to event guests.

Such was the case at the Fairmont Pittsburgh hotel, named Fairmont Hotels & Resorts' 2013 Hotel of the Year and host venue for the company's 2014 General Managers Conference. Local Fairmont leaders sought to showcase regional cuisine and culture as part of a welcoming reception for conference participants. Conscious of the public's demand for healthier food options, hoteliers and restaurateurs have enthusiastically embraced the "farm-to-table" concept. At Fairmont Pittsburgh, local food vendors have become important partners in the constant quest to achieve culinary excellence. Many of these vendors were invited to participate in the welcoming reception event at the Fairmont, where the farm-to-table trend became the impetus for a unique design presentation that showcased the history, culture and cuisine of Pittsburgh and its surroundings.

Working with Fairmont chefs, who created the event menu based on locally-sourced food providers, we developed displays for reception hors d'oeuvres to showcase Pittsburgh's "Steel City" moniker in combination with a more rustic, rural look. Instead of wooden tables that you might expect to see in farm-to-table events or restaurants, we assembled a combination of metal tables made from a mix of industrial metals: galvanized and brushed steel, aluminum, and a textured pressed metal alloy. We used metal as a nod to Pittsburgh's history as a steel town. Display tables featured local meats, breads and cheeses on carving boards, while servers passed trays of light bites, each resting atop a serving skewer stuck into live wheat grass. Single-serving dessert items were displayed on tiered trays adapted from rustic retail display cases lined with vintage food and agriculture advertisements. With Pittsburgh's history of German immigrants, pretzels were featured prominently in the decadent multi-chocolate dessert items. A presentation of specialty teas from a regional tea company were served in clear glass pots on pedestals.

- Sala...
- Pork...
- Hea...
- Am...
- Whole ... Herbal Mustard
- Dijon
- Picked Mustard Seed
- Jager Jell-O
- House Smoked Atlantic Salmon

CREAMERIES OF
PENNSYLVANIA

Local Artisan
Cheese Selection

& • Red Bamboo Honey
• Apple Preserve
• Red Pepper Jelly

Roasted

Pickled
Mustard Seed

Throughout the room, design accents included vintage baskets and terra cotta pots with live plants, some presented under glass. Sunflowers, grasses and wildflowers added to the room's rustic elements. A custom bar was constructed using the cut-off ends of more than a dozen wooden wine crates, all attached to the galvanized steel façade. In keeping with the organic theme, fresh wheat grass, green moss and hanging green amaranthus grew from each of the wooden wine crates. A brushed metal wall behind the bar featured more than twenty display boxes, many supporting tall bottles made from orange-tinted glass, along with more wildflowers and greens. Overhead displays referenced menu items below and mimiced old-world posters featuing illustrations of food items such as local cheeses, fish and baked goods. Wooden crate displays hung overhead from chains connected to the ceiling; the chains also suspended scaffolding with overhead lighting. At this memorable event, executives from around the world came to Pittsburgh, where they were treated to many of the region's tastes and sights, as well as its culture and history.

Specialty
TEAS

·Kea Lani
Orange Pineapple
(Cold in a cocktail)

·House Blend
(Served Hot)

·Fairmont Earl Grey
(Black Tea)

·Fairmont Digestif
(Wellness Tea)

·Kyoto Cherry Rose
(Green Tea)

How to set
MILKING
to music

Dividers help to create intimate areas within a large room. Here, we used wood frames with bunched aluminum screen, which has a nice texture. The window screen material looks great in full daylight, but displays even more dramatically after dark when uplit with colored light.

Pedestals atop dowell rods rising up from a bed of wheat grass showcased the various flavors of tea, which were smartly presented in clear pots.

Menu

SUSTAINABLY SOURCED SEAFOOD

Maple Cured Salmon Bacon
served with:
- Sweet Corn Salsa
- Summer Radish
- Scallions

Cast Seared Lake Erie Walleye
served with:
- Olive Braised Tomato Fondue
- Green Onion Chimichurri
- Veal Jus

The history of the region was emphasized in the signage for this event. A combination of antique illustrations, historic local plot maps and property deeds were used to embellish the menus and food station decor. We trimmed the signs in wood, accented with inexpensive thumb tacks.

CORNER BAKERY

Offerings from and in the style of famous local creations.

- Sarris Chocolate
- Clarke Bar
- Tea Infused Desserts
- Burnt Almond Cupcakes
- Klondike Bars

Vintage newspaper ads were revealed beneath desserts that guests selected from wooden display bins. Pretzels were an ingredient chosen as representative of Pittsburgh's German immigrant population.

By creating custom trays for passed hors d'oeuvres, we bring focus to the food. The surprise of an interesting presentation engages guests, sparks conversation and shows our careful attention to detail.

PARTY TO LIFE

Inspiration for event design is not a one way street; the ideas shouldn't all come from the event designer. Creating a successful concept is often a matter of inspiring clients to share their ideas, which can provide a good foundation for the designer to build upon.

The most successful event planners also possess a good sense of psychology, especially when it comes to getting into the psyches of their clients. Clients usually come to their first meetings with excitement and anticipation about the event they hope to host. It's best to match your client's energy level, in order to establish an early bond and impart a sense of companionship. Too much enthusiasm from an event designer could intimidate a client; too little could frustrate them. Be sure to provide a comfortable, inviting environment for your first meeting, to maximize opportunities for inspiration. Open your meeting with a brief recap of why you're there. Let them do the talking. It's important to be a good listener. Asking the right questions is also important. "What do you want to achieve?" "How do you want your guests to feel?" "What should they experience?" For a corporate event, be sure to ask, "What messages are you trying to share?"

Hopefully, you'll develop a bond much like one we have established with a gentleman and devoted client who asked us to create an 80th birthday party. "I want to celebrate life," he said. That was enough to get the wheels turning, to provide the inspiration for the creation of a "tree of life" in the entry foyer of the country club where the birthday party was held. Multiple iron tree structures were pulled together as the foundation for the tree of life, with woody vines wrapped around the iron branches. Large leaves suspended from ribbons became place cards, with the name of each guest and corresponding table number on one side, and a meaningful quote about life written in calligraphy on the reverse. The tree of life was a unique and creative way to welcome our clients' special guests. It stood five feet high above a lobby table and spread out seven feet wide. The walls of the foyer were covered in photographs blown up and assembled into montages of family and friends, as well as historic family photographs, some of which included the guest of honor. The montages surprised and delighted party guests, who were immediately reunited with others pictured in the photographs.

The ballroom became a regal party showplace, where gold, white and blue hues came together under a ceiling decorated with individual strands of square, gold Mylar sequins. A tall candelabra was used as a stand to hold an inverted lampshade accented with individual gold metallic confetti pieces nestled on a bed of white lilies, orchids, calla lilies and green amaranthus. Large custom rings were created to sit high in the air and encompass the gold candlesticks, pillar candles and flowers. Calla lilies lined the rings to add emphasis to the circular pattern. Four distinct linen styles covered a combination of round and long tables, which were arranged around a raised, white dancefloor, reflecting lights from dozens of overhead fixtures. Confetti and confetti-like graphics were a major component of the event design, which picked up on the use of confetti as part of the invitations. Departing guests received specially-labeled bottles of wine. Each of the wine labels also included this meaningful quote about life: "Gratitude is happiness doubled by wonder." It was a fitting farewell message for a remarkable celebration of life.

The entrance was designed to honor a lifetime with friends and family. Photos were prominently displayed surrounding the "Tree of Life" placecard display. Place cards, each inscribed with a meaningful quote, hung from the branches.

When planning an event that we know will put a strain on the catering staff, we like to bring in our own team to help with the service. In this event the group passed wine and hors d'oeuvres during the cocktail hour and were dressed in bright yellow. Later, they changed into navy blue and white for serving in the ballroom. The in-house service staff wore custom printed ties to coordinate.

Strolling seafood trays are perfect for the cocktail hour. Using them has two benefits: it minimizes the amount of seafood that has to be ordered and you eliminate the large buffet style seafood display that is sitting out and constantly needs to be re-iced.

Custom service trays never fail to delight guests. People always comment on the unique items. It's that type of reaction that makes an event memorable.

Adding hints of gold to the flatware, crystal and china brought the entire tablescape together and it all shined beautifully in the candlelight.

The metal circles that provided the foundation for the floral arrangements seen here were fabricated in our shop. We were able to use them as tall centerpieces as well as in low groupings lining the center of the long tables. As you looked out across the room, the tall structures made a dramatic visual at mid-height in the empty area between the elaborate tables and ceiling treatment above.

Towers that flanked the stage were also made of the gold confetti garlands. If you look closely you can see that we repeated the confetti pattern at the top of the table signs and on the printed menus at each place setting.

Using different china patterns throughout the meal gives each course personality.

As guests were entertained in the ballroom, we turned the "Tree of Life" place card display into the favor table. A carefully selected bottle of Cabernet was a great celebratory gift for guests to take as they exited this very special event.

TOAST THE HOST

As a psychological phenomenon, inspiration is often complex and multi-dimensional. Inspiration can come in a flash or develop over time. It can come because you look for it, or it can come when you least expect it. It can come from one momentary impression, or from a combination of stimuli. Such was the case with an event we call the "Plastic Party." In this case, our guest of honor happened to be a plastics manufacturer, who owns factories that stamp out tens of thousands of inexpensive plastic items every day. This was the man, who, as a child, took to heart the advice given to Dustin Hoffman's character in the 1967 movie, "The Graduate," when he was told the future was in plastics.

Fast forward a half century to a birthday party planned by the family of our plastics executive and guest of honor. His immediate family desired to congratulate him with a small dinner party for only 12 close friends and family members. Our first meeting identified plastics as an important personal point of reference. From there, it was easy to identify potential plastic design elements that could be utilized to create a unique and memorable party setting.

We began with walls made of thousands of small plastic glasses, all glued to display boards that could be assembled in advance and then brought in prior to the party so they could be attached en masse to the party room walls. We created chandeliers from hundreds of plastic champagne glasses, all glued at their bases and attached to large clear plastic balls. Metal stems of bendable conduit were added to each plastic chandelier ball, to create the effect of giant plastic dandelions. Inserted into dozens of the champagne glasses were small, round "Fairy Berries," which glow on and off and have a magical look. At the base of the plastic chandeliers were shiny metal balls in patterns of silver, white and blue circles and squares. These were complemented by votive candles and calla lilies with mirrored and metal table surfaces and smooth silverware designed to reinforce the sleek style that comes with an intense display of plastic.

Guests were seated on chiavari chairs with open backs to show off their clear plastic construction. The table, itself, was custom made of aluminum and steel. An assortment of entrees matched each guest's dinner preference with the menu of his or her choice. Reaction of party guests and the guest of honor was a combination of amazement and enjoyment. There is something surreal about creating a beautiful and elegant event out of something that is not normally considered beautiful or elegant. With the right inspiration, it's possible to make the ordinary extraordinary, memorable and meaningful.

The soft glow produced by hundreds of Fairy Berries made the giant dandelion flowers seem alive. The small LED lights, which were glued inside the plastic glasses, illuminated at various times then subtly faded away.

The meal began with individual servings of tabbouleh, marinated olives, roasted garlic and hummus with pita. We chose to use the most contemporary china and flatware possible. This unexpected shape coexhists nicely with the other textures and elements of the design.

DISK-O SIX-O

Sometimes, inspiration is right in front of you. For two years, a neon green, flexible and flat, 10-inch nylon disc hung pinned to a bulletin board at the office. Team members commented on it, noticing it at first, then gradually becoming accustomed to its presence, even though its neon green color screamed, "Don't forget me! Use me for event décor!" It was only a matter of time before the right opportunity emerged. We had picked up the sample disc at an annual event trade show, where so many good ideas and props can be found. We walk those trade show aisles with a goal of adding to our bag of tricks. Event industry product vendors offer so many unique items. It's our job to spot them and figure out how to maximize the potential for event décor, design, and production.

14,000 nylon discs later, we connected and configured this item into a color explosion that set the scene inside an arena that played host to 500 guests at a one-of-a-kind birthday party. In addition to neon green, the discs were in neon hues of orange, yellow, blue and pink, and each with a thin black edge. Once we devised a way to connect the disks with special clips, they were arranged in color waves that we used to create individual strands, which, when placed together made multi-colored sheets of disks. When suspended, the sheets of disks became lightweight, easily erected walls, which made visually impactful temporary event architecture inside the vast space.

The arena seating rising up from either side of the party floor was camouflaged with black velvet. Ten 40-foot long walls of the nylon discs and 14-foot tall nylon disc towers were then strategically placed to create the perfect party environment for this spectacular surprise. The event centerpiece was a 20-foot by 20-foot by 40-foot high chandelier of connected discs suspended above the enormous four sided bar, which was located in the center of the arena. Air flow caused the hanging strands to slowly sway and rotate while they changed hue under multi-colored lights. This dramatic chandelier provided weight to the center of the party floor and its subtle movement was an unexpected benefit.

The party and the décor weren't entirely about nylon discs. Entertainment never stopped. The 500 guests' voices in a chorus of "Surprise!" as the guest of honor entered the party were only the beginning of a night full of excitement. Fire-breathing bartenders thrilled party guests by mixing cocktails in a choreographed routine, as did go-go dancers in raised cages flanking the dance floor. Disco-inspired stilt walkers wearing custom designed pants made of thousands of multi- colored strips of ribbon and crowned by huge neon afro wigs could be seen high above the crowd. They dangled trays of hors d'oeuvres down to guests below.

Five food stations featured scallops, risotto, seafood and sushi, pizza and salad. Each station was designed as an individual kitchen and built out on the arena floor; they were complete with refrigeration, ovens and heat lamps. Nothing was cooked in advance; all cooking was done on the floor in sight of the guests by a team of thirty chefs.

Shiny pots and pans decorated the food station upper levels, where musicians in custom costumes worked as chefs in view of the party crowd. To the delight of spectators, the "chefs" spontaneously performed percussion jam sessions using their spatulas and utensils upon purposefully placed pots and pans as though they were drum sets. A dance troupe entertained party guests with three different numbers, including "Stayin' Alive" from the movie "Saturday Night Fever," performed in white disco suits a la John Travolta. Not coincidentally, the graphic identity of the event, as well as the digital dance floor, featured a caricature of the guest of honor in a similar Travolta-esque costume. A fully costumed 1970s theme band took the stage and brought the dance floor to life, playing the classic dance hits of the era. At the bar area, a flash mob of more than 50 people came together suddenly to undertake an ambush style dance number directed at the birthday boy. He hardly caught his breath before a 6-foot tall birthday cake rolled into view; the theme from Jaws was a humorous accompaniment as the threatening cake located its prey in the heart of the party crowd. Once it found its mark, out popped the sexy female singer who performed a sultry rendition of "Hey Big Spender."

Rolling dessert carts that featured graphics of sexy lips eating delectable treats were pushed through the crowd by hostesses wearing full skirts made of hundreds of colorful napkins. Party guests were invited to peel off a napkin one at a time. The ladies were complemented by delivery guys peddling a bicycle-powered ice cream cart stocked with cool treats. When guests exited after a night packed full of nonstop entertainment, their party favor was an individual custom cake displayed in an incredible custom 1970s conversion van. The metallic multi-color flames and cherry red shag rug interior were another thrill in a night jam packed with surprises. All in all, this party was a visual masterpiece, and all of it was built around that one simple nylon disc.

Fully functioning kitchens were designed and built on the hockey arena floor. Food was prepared on site in full view of guests throughout the evening. This action element gave the event energy and excitement. Food was always hot and fresh. Guests enjoyed feeling like they were stopping by various little restaurants.

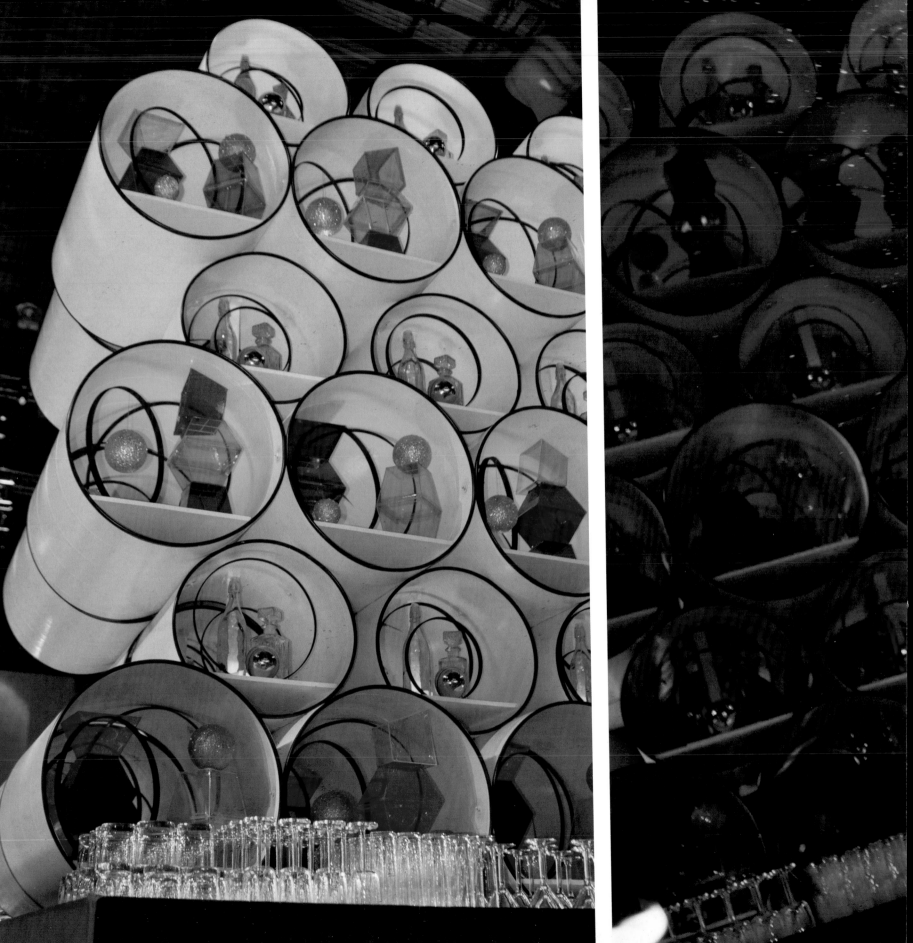

Massive contemporary floral centerpieces comprised of tropical and exotic flowers towered above the tables and seating areas in modern white urns. The unexpected addition of disco balls to the structured arrangements kept the design on theme.

Dessert walls are a great concept to use for conserving space in a crowded event. Rather than have a large stationary dessert display, these walls wheel treats out to the guests in an unexpected way, then can be taken to the back to be refilled with goodies as needed. The bold graphics make a strong visual impact when they enter a room and can be recreated for each event theme.

Costumed event actors bring the party to life by giving it personality. We often hire the same actors for multiple events. When we find someone who is both visually interesting and also has a personality that guests respond to, we keep their information on hand in a talent folder that includes a photo, a description, their measurements and any special skills they may bring to the table.

Local theaters are a great resource for finding people that are more than just a pretty face. Modeling agencies are good when you need beauty, but I tend to find that guests respond to trained performers best. Trained actors are fearless about getting into character and engaging their audiences. An enthusiastic actor can really sell the event.

As guests exited the building, they were treated to one last surprise, a classic 1970s conversion van that displayed the custom cake party favors. The auto show award winner created a special exit and a last look back to the disco era. What you can't see in the photo is the interior red shag carpeting!

ACKNOWLEDGMENTS

How do I begin to thank everyone who has had a part in making this book a reality? It was a labor of love not only for me but for our clients, the team, the vendor partners, and my friends and family.

Thank you to every single person who helped me bring my vision for each of the events in the book to life.

To my loyal clients, who so often become my friends, thank you for letting me be a part of your most important moments and special memories. Especially Flora Cafaro, who was and will always be my favorite client. She gave me a chance 30 years ago, and has stuck with me over so many years.

To my team, past and present, you are and have always been the backbone of the company. It is your fearless passion that allows me to create the most wonderful experiences. There have been many of you over thirty years and I truly thank each and every one of you.

To Maribeth Farcas, head of production, and Stephanie Strudwick, head of the art department, you both have been a huge part of the success of our company over these many years we've been together. Thank you for your constant support and tremendous contributions.

To all of the colleagues and partners with whom I have had the pleasure to work over so many years, we have been a powerful team. We have stood by one another. We have helped each other be the best we can be, one event at a time. Thank you all.

Thank you to all my friends and family who have showered me with love and support, who have weathered the storms, through thick and thin. Especially, to my mother, whose prayers have kept me healthy and safe. Your love has always been a reminder of how lucky I am.

To Anna, my sister, my business partner, my friend, you and I have been through it all over the last 30 years! Through the laughs and through the tears, through the ups and the downs, we have survived and become stronger people, stronger bosses, and stronger as brother and sister. I love you.

To Eska, who has been the major force behind this book, but more than that behind the brand of Joe Mineo Creative. You have helped me see the potential in what we have created, given me courage to step beyond my comfort zone and to see in me what I could not see in myself. Thank you for all your support and love, as a major part of my team and as my friend.

Lastly, I thank the person who puts a smile on my face every day, my husband Gary. I have waited for you all of my life and at 50 years old you appeared. Thank you for agreeing to be my ghost writer for the book and helping me to express my thoughts like no one else could. For giving so much time and having patience with it, focusing on every word, sentence and paragraph. Gary, you are the love of my life.

One more, thank you God ... He knows why.

BOOK ACKNOWLEDGMENTS
Author - Joe Mineo, *Writing* - Gary Bitner, *Design and Writing Collaborator* - Eska Bauman Paumier,
Graphic Design & Cover Design - Justin Banasiewicz, *Editing Assistant* - Alison Quinn Cox,
Cover Photo and Author Portrait - Nathan Migal

CHAPTER CONTRIBUTIONS

In Party Fashion
Photos - New Image, *Venue* - Landerhaven, *Lighting* - Vincent Lighting Systems, *Seamster* - W. Rick Schilling,
Graphic Design - Stephanie Moore Strudwick, *Linens* - Joe Mineo Creative, *Rentals* - Event Source Party and Equipment
Rentals, *Catering* - Executive Caterers

In The Drawing Room
Photos - Nathan Migal, *Drawings* - W. Rick Schilling, *Graphic Design* -Ashley Vaughn, *Lighting* - Solus Lighting Ltd,
Linens - Mosaic, Inc., *Rentals* - Event Source Party and Equipment Rentals, *Pastries* - The Cake Boutique

Give Them Chills
Photos - Nathan Migal, *Venue* - Stambaugh Auditorium, *Lighting* - Vincent Lighting Systems,
Linens - Joe Mineo Creative, *Rentals* - Event Source Party and Equipment Rentals, *Cake* - The Cake Boutique

Silver Screen Soirée
Photos - Nathan Migal, *Lighting* - Solus Lighting Ltd., *Rentals* - Event Source Party and Equipment Rental,
Linens - Joe Mineo Creative

Inspired Fête
Photos - Nathan Migal, *Venue* - Anne K. Christman Memorial Hall; Stambaugh Auditorium, *Lighting* - Solus Lighting Ltd.,
Rentals - Event Source Party and Equipment Rentals, *Graphic Design* - Ashley Vaughn

Once In A Lifetime
Photos - Araujo Photo, *Lighting* - 42Inc., *Cake* - White Flower, *Linens* - Joe Mineo Creative, *Rentals* - D.C. Rental, Event
Source Party and Equipment Rentals, *Caterer* - Leo's Ristorante, *Lead Floral Designer* - Pam Clark

It's About Time
Photos - John Altdorfer, *Event Management* - Joe Mineo Creative: Eska Bauman-Paumier, *Lighting* - Colortone Staging and
Rentals, *Custom Animation for Video Projection* - SimCoach Games : Adam Chizmar, *Window Graphics* - Endagraph, *Graphic
Design* - Tara Wray and Eska Bauman Paumier, *Printing* - Copies At Carson, Bud's Signs and Jones and Associates, *Rentals*
- Event Source Party and Equipment Rentals, and All Occasions Party Rental, *Linen's* - Mosaic Inc., *Makeup Artist* - Eve
Negley, *Entertainment* - Cello Fury, West Coast Music: The Cowling Band, *Performance* - Cirque Mechanics: Gantry Bike,
Dance - Point Park University Dance Department, *Choreography* - Kiesha Lalama, *Catering* - Levy Restaurants, *Pastries* -
Bella Christie and Lil Z's Sweet Boutique, *Venue* - David L. Lawrence Convention Center

Unlike Any Other
Photos - Joey Kennedy, *Church* - St. Patrick's Hubbard Ohio, *Invitations* - Richard's Notebook, *Reception Venue* - Stambaugh
Auditorium, *Make Up Artist* - The Makeup Boutique: Jen Melia, *Rentals* - Event Source Party and Equipment Rentals,
Be Seated, Special Events Party Rental, and All Occasions Party Rental, *Linens* - Mosaic Inc., *Lighting* - Vincent Lighting
Systems, *Painter* - Agnes Csiszar Russo, *Actors* - Jeff Peterson and Krysta Sylvester, *Cakes* - Blue Iris

Game On
Photos - Phil Goldman Photography, Eska Bauman Paumier, *Venue* - Landerhaven, *Lighting* -Hughie's Event Production, *Graphic Design* - Eska Bauman Paumier, *Rentals* - Event Source Party and Equipment Rentals, *Carpentry* - Marty Chill

Rock The Party
Photos - Nathan Migal, *Venue* - The Cleveland Public Auditorium and Confrence Center, *Graphic Design* - Eska Bauman Paumier, *Stage Production* - HBO, *Linens* - L'Nique Linens, *Rentals* - Event Source Party and Equipment Rentals, *Models* - Taxi Talent Management, *Grafitti Airbrush Artist* - Airtistix: Josh Shaull, *Lighting* - Vincent Lighting Systems

Life Changing Event
Photos - David Cartee, *Event Management* - Party People: Pat Butto, *Venue* - Beechmont Country Club, *Tenting* - Lasting Impressions, *Lighting* - Vincent Lighting Systems, *Cake* - White Flower, *Linens and Chair Covers* - Wildflower Linens, *Menu* - So Bella Design Studio

It's My Party
Photos - Nathan Migal, *Lighting* - Vincent Lighting Systems, *Venue* - Stambaugh Auditorium, *Linen's* - L'Nique Linens, *Rentals* - Event Source Party and Equipment Rental, *Catering* - Leo's Ristorante, *Graphic Design* - Eska Bauman Paumier, *Dance* - Fred Astaire Dance Studio: Youngstown, Ohio

Local Flavor
Photos - Joey Kennedy, *Venue* - Fairmont Hotel Pittsburgh Pennsylvania, *Lighting* - Fairmont Hotel, *Graphic Design* - Ashley Vaughn and Eska Bauman Paumier, *Furniture* - Joe Mineo Creative

Party To Life
Photos - Marc and Tony Photography, *Venue* - Beechmont Country Club, *Lighting* - Solus Lighting Ltd, *Actors* - Gina Mineo and Corey Farcas, *Rentals* - Event Source Party and Equipment Rentals, *Linens* - Mosaic Inc, *Entertainment* - Dean Martin and Friends: Tom Stevens, The Four Freshman

Toast The Host
Photos - Nathan Migal, *Lighting* - Solus Lighting Ltd, *Graphic Design* - Tara Wray, *Rentals* - Event Source Party and Equipment Rental

Disk-O Six-O
Photos - Araujo Photo, *Lighting* - Colortone Staging and Rentals, *Catering* - Leo's Ristorante, *Bar Tender Performers*- Flair Bartenders:Robbie Flair, *Graphic Design* - Eska Bauman Paumier, *Actors* - Edward Bryan, Kala Marie Craig, Ra'Neeka Starling, David Munnell, *Linens* - Mosaic Inc., *Rentals* - Event Source Party and Equipment Rentals, *Catering* - Leo's Ristorante, *Dancers*- Fred Astaire Dance Studio Youngstown, Ohio, *Band* - Boogie Wonder Band, *Performer* - Dal Bouey